Narratives of Indian Captivities

A Narrative of the Captivity of Nehemiah How in 1745-1747

Victor Hugo Paltsits

HERITAGE BOOKS
2016

HERITAGE BOOKS
AN IMPRINT OF HERITAGE BOOKS, INC.

Books, CDs, and more—Worldwide

For our listing of thousands of titles see our website
at
www.HeritageBooks.com

A Facsimile Reprint
Published 2016 by
HERITAGE BOOKS, INC.
Publishing Division
5810 Ruatan Street
Berwyn Heights, Md. 20740

Copyright © 1904 The Burrows Brothers Company

— Publisher's Notice —
In reprints such as this, it is often not possible to remove blemishes from the original. We feel the contents of this book warrant its reissue despite these blemishes and hope you will agree and read it with pleasure.

International Standard Book Numbers
Paperbound: 978-0-7884-4082-3
Clothbound: 978-0-7884-6429-4

CONTENTS

	PAGE
INTRODUCTION, *Victor Hugo Paltsits*	. 7
HOW'S NARRATIVE	. 23
Facsimile of original title-page .	. 25
INDEX	. 61

INTRODUCTION

THE present town of Putney, Windham County, Vermont, is situated on the west bank of the Connecticut River. It extends for a distance of five miles from north to south, and stretches between six and seven miles from its eastern to its western boundary. In the easterly part of the town, formed by a large bend in the river, the Great Meadow is located, and comprises about five hundred acres. Its soil has always yielded easily to cultivation, rewarding industry with an abundant crop of hay or various kinds of grain. Originally the surrounding forests were overgrown with beach, elm, maple, butternut and oak trees, while the lowest part of the meadow abounded with a tangled growth of yellow pine, and the steep hills on the west were covered with white pines of huge growth.* This region, we may believe, was early inhabited by the aborigines, if flint arrow-heads, spears, broken pots and other Indian remains are evidence of their habitat; but whether they were permanent or merely occasional residents has not been determined.

In 1735-6, the Massachusetts-Bay government, cognizant from bitter experience of the

---

*For the topographical description I am indebted to the accounts by Rev. Amos Foster, and David L. Mansfield, in Hemenway's *Vermont Historical Gazetteer*, vol. v, pp. 217-222, 250-251.

disasters from Indian incursions at the westward, determined to establish a chain of fortified settlements in the valley of the Connecticut. Willing settlers were gradually procured through the encouragement of governmental land-grants, and presumably in 1738 or 1739 the occupation of the Great Meadow and No. 2 (now Westmoreland, N. H.), across the river, was begun. Nehemiah How, of Grafton, Mass., William Phips, David Rugg, of Lancaster, Mass., their families, together with Robert Baker and others, made the first clearing in the Great Meadow, and built a fort in the central part, called Fort Hill. Daniel How, nephew of Nehemiah, also a captive at Quebec during a part of the war, with Thomas Crisson and others from Rutland, Mass., cleared the ground at No. 2, built themselves log-huts and depended for protection on the neighboring fort, to the building of which they had contributed.* In a few years these intrepid pioneers, by the dint of assiduity, succeeded in transforming the primeval meadows and uplands to conditions favorable for vegetation and pasturage, and gathered a good stock of cattle. Yet latent horrors of Indian warfare lay beneath the apparent tranquillity of these years of peace. The first depredation by the Indians in the Connecticut valley, during King George's war, was on the Great Meadow.

---

*N. H. Town Papers, vol. xiii (1884), pp. 652-653.

INTRODUCTION 9

On July 5th, 1745, William Phips was hoeing in his cornfield, in the southwest corner of the meadow, when suddenly two Indians surprised him, and led him away captive to the woods — a distance of near half a mile. They halted in order to permit one of them to descend a steep hill, where he had left something. Phips, with great strategic ingenuity, seizing the moment when the remaining Indian was off his guard, struck him down with his hoe and "chop'd him very much," so that he died soon thereafter. Snatching this Indian's gun, he shot and killed the second Indian as he was returning. Phips then took to his heels, but was almost instantly killed by a shot from one of the guns of three other Indians, who appeared on the spot at this juncture. They scalped him and "mangled his body in a most Inhuman manner." The news of this outbreak brought Capt. Ebenezer Alexander with a company of fifty-six men to the region, and they were kept in service scouting the woods and guarding the towns, from July 12th until September 8th.* There was a brief lull in the exhibitions of savagery,

---

*Doolittle's *Short Narrative Of Mischief done by the French and Indian Enemy, on the Western Frontiers Of the Province of the Massachusetts-Bay.* Boston, 1750, p. 2; Rev. John Taylor's "Appendix" to Rev. John Williams's *Redeemed Captive returning to Zion.* Sixth edition. Boston, 1795, p. 114; *N. E. Hist. and Gen. Register,* vol. ix, p. 163, from Hampshire County Recorder's Book; Temple and Sheldon's *Hist. of Northfield, Mass.,* pp. 240-241; Hemenway's *Vermont Hist. Gazetteer,* vol. v, pp. 219, 252.

but on October 11th, 1745,* the Great Meadow was infested anew.

On this "black Friday" morning Nehemiah How walked a distance of "about 50 Rods" or a little over one-sixth of a mile from the fort, for the purpose of cutting some wood. He had completed his task and was returning to the fort, but had proceeded only a few paces, when suddenly he heard "the crackling of Fences" behind him and, looking back in the direction whence the noise came, "saw 12 or 13 Indians, with red painted Heads," running after him. Starting on a run, he shouted desperately, hoping thereby to attract the attention of the guard at the fort. The fleet-footed Indians, however, overtook him by the time he had gone ten rods. They seized him; led him away to a "swamp," probably where the creek now is, and there his captors bound him. The Indians, who were a party of Abenakis of St. Francis,† and numbered about fifty,‡ were in the meadow scarce an hour, but in that time made a futile attack on the fort, and created havoc among the cattle in the

---

*The dates are all according to "old style," in use by the English, unless otherwise designated.

†*Collection de Manuscrits relatifs à la Nouvelle-France*, vol. iii, p. 268.

‡Deacon Noah Wright, in a letter written to his brother from Deerfield, on October 27th, 1745, says the sentry at the fort, when attacked, told him there were about fifty Indians in the whole party.—*N. E. Hist. and Gen. Register*, vol. ii (1848), p. 207. The Hampshire County Recorder's Book, in *N. E. Hist. and Gen. Register*, vol. ix, p. 163, gives their number erroneously as "about fourscore French and Indians."

field. Deacon Noah Wright, who arrived in the scout sent out, found "such things to behold as wold raise the passions of the most steddy man in the world." Cattle which the Indians had butchered and hides lay "spred almost over the ground." As they went through the meadow, the scouting party could scarce turn their eyes "without seeing ded creatures sum with their guts tore ought & some ript open & others part of them carried off & a grat many that lay untouched ondly their hyds were taken off."* From the deposition which How made to the French at Quebec, we learn that the fort was commanded by a lieutenant, and contained twenty soldiers and ten others when attacked.† During the retreat one of the Indians was killed by a shot from the fort; another was so mortally wounded that he died "fourteen Days" after their arrival in Canada, and a third, who had hold of How, had a bullet shot through his powder-horn.

How was liberated from the "swamp" and led to a spot "about half a Mile" and "in open Sight of the Fort." Passing along the west bank of the Connecticut River, about three miles in a northerly direction from the fort, they observed two men in a canoe, paddling down the river near the opposite shore, below "Taylor's Island." They were David Rugg

---

*Noah Wright, in *N. E. Hist. and Gen. Reg.*, vol. ii, pp. 207-208.
†*Coll. de MSS.*, vol. iii, pp. 268-270.

and Robert Baker. Right speedily "twenty or thirty Guns" were discharged at them. Rugg was killed instantly in the canoe, but Baker succeeded in gaining his safety with some difficulty by reaching the shore. Some of the Indians swam the stretch of the river, and returned with the canoe to inflict upon the warm corpse of Rugg the indignities of the scalping-knife. Proceeding for another mile by the river side, they halted at a house. At the same time How's son, Caleb, together with Jonathan Thayer and Samuel Nutting, were spied by the Indians running along the bank, and five of them gave chase to head them off. Fortunately they escaped, presumably by means of secreting themselves "under the Bank of the River." The Indians continued northward until they arrived at Black River, in the environs of Fort No. 4, now Charlestown, N. H. They then struck out to cross the mountain wilderness of the present state of Vermont; probably came as far as what is now Larrabee's Point, opposite Fort Ticonderoga; continued to Crown Point, and embarked for Quebec, through Lake Champlain and the rivers Sorel and St. Lawrence. We may accept How's own testimony that he was not subjected to any severe cruelties by his Indian captors, who generally were kind to him. Only at Chambly was he maltreated by some Iroquois whom he encountered. In this he fared far better from these heartless sons of

INTRODUCTION 13

the forest, than most of his countrymen in times of conflict.*

As soon as the assault on the Great Meadow was communicated to Northfield, Ensign Stratton set out with ten men for Fort Dummer. On the afternoon of the same day, Saturday, October 19th, twenty-nine men left Deerfield; marched through Northfield, and joined the former party at Fort Dummer, at ten o'clock that night. Meanwhile Col. Josiah Willard had gone to the Great Meadow, taking with him as many men of his garrison as could be spared. The forty others followed on Sunday morning, and arrived at the Great Meadow about two o'clock in the afternoon. Willard had just left with his men, and they were therefore ordered to follow. They soon came up with the advance party and, after gaining what information they could from those at the fort, the whole scout, consisting of ninety-four men, began the march. They followed the tracks of the Indians until about sunset of the 20th, camped, and on Monday morning, the 21st, started for Fort No. 4, stripping themselves on the way for battle. When they arrived at No. 4 the enemy had departed from the region. Lodging that night at the fort, they began their homeward march on the next morning, October 22d; proceeded by way of Upper Ashuelot (Keene, N. H.),

---

*His testimony appears in his pamphlet and in his deposition at Quebec.

INTRODUCTION

and arrived in Northfield on Wednesday, October 23d.*

In March, 1747, thirty or forty Indians attempted to burn Shattuck's Fort, between Northfield and Col. Hinsdale's Fort. They were pursued on the 31st from Northfield by Capt. Eleazer Melvin and his company, as far as the Great Meadow, but the Indians succeeded in burning the fort which the English had deserted.†

The deserted region of the Great Meadow began to be resettled in February, 1755, and in the early part of that year the few new settlers built another fort, in the southeast part of the meadow. A town charter had been granted in advance from New Hampshire, dated December 26th, 1753.

During the dispute with New York over territorial domain, that colony gave the town a charter, dated November 6th, 1766. The town was organized and the first town officers chosen, on May 8th, 1770.‡ Its subsequent history has been steady and honorable, but historic instinct must ever accord a high place to the sturdy pioneers who laid the foundation stones of its superstructure.

---

*This analysis is given with particularity from Noah Wright, in *N. E. Hist. and Gen. Register*, vol. ii, pp. 207-208, because misinterpreted to some extent in Hemenway's *Gazetteer*, vol. v, p. 253, and Temple and Sheldon's *Hist. of Northfield*, p. 241.

†Doolittle, p. 11, Cf. conflicting statements in Hemenway, vol. v, pp. 219, 252.

‡Hemenway, pp. 220-221.

BIBLIOGRAPHY

Three narratives by New England captives, during the Five Years' French and Indian war, run parallel so far as their common residence in Quebec is concerned. They were written by Nehemiah How, Rev. John Norton, chaplain of Fort Massachusetts, and Captain William Pote, Jr., master of the schooner *Montague*, in the employ of the Massachusetts-Bay government. The small but now excessively rare pamphlets of How and Norton were both printed in the year 1748, while the very extensive and by far more important journal of Pote, lay in manuscript until its first publication in 1896. There are numerous discrepancies of a day or two in the dates of deaths as recorded by these three diarists, but I am inclined generally to favor the earliest date as the true one, because it seems likely that each of them recorded in his diary as soon as he received the information. They exhibit, however, other vagaries as, for example, mistakes in personal and place nomenclature, while the three accounts supplement each other as to material facts.

It is, no doubt, a patent fact that very much of the earlier editing of American historical texts was performed in a faulty manner, judged by modern critical methods. This we have found to be particularly true of the *Indian Captivities* collected by Samuel G. Drake, and first printed for him in 1839. But we are not to despise pioneer efforts in the landmarks of our historical work, even if our verdict is against their present service. Drake, be it said to his honor, saved from oblivion much that might otherwise have been gnawed by the tooth of time, and his work created an interest in a field which he made peculiarly his own. In the above-mentioned collection he presented the first and only reprint of How's pamphlet which has appeared up to the present edition. He also reprinted for the first time an annotated text of Norton's work, as an appendix to his *Particular History of the Five Years' French and Indian War,* published at Boston in 1870. At the same time he reissued one hundred copies separately, with new pagination and a copy of the original title-page.

In reprinting How's pamphlet we have had recourse to a fine uncut copy in the New York Public Library (Lenox Library Building). It was purchased at the first Brinley sale, in 1879, item 481, for twenty-five dollars, and the autograph of the Rev. Dr. Edward Wigglesworth on the title-page, shows that he owned it in 1748, the year of its publication. As this tract seldom appears in the market, and as the demand for original early Indian captivities is great, it would be hazardous to guess a particular figure which so fine a copy might fetch to-day. The following analytical collation is presented for the service of collectors and bibliographers:

A | NARRATIVE | Of the Captivity | OF | Nehemiah How, | Who was taken by the Indians at the *Great-| Meadow Fort* above *Fort-Dummer*, where he was | an Inhabitant, *October* 11*th* 1745. | Giving an Account of what he met with in his | travelling to *Canada*, and while he was in Prifon | there. | Together with an Account of Mr. *HOW's* Death | at *Canada*. | [*Quotation from Psalm cxxxvii*] |

BOSTON : *N. E.* | Printed and Sold oppofite to the Prifon in Queen– | Street. 1748. |

Printed page measures 5¾ in. height, by 3¼ in. width; title, verso blank; "A Narrative, &c.," pp. 3-22; "The Names of the Subfcribers," pp. (2). Signatures : A—C in fours.

GENEALOGY

Nehemiah How belonged to a worthy family of Massachusetts Puritans.* His grandfather, John How or Howe, was a son of John How, Esq., who it is supposed lived in Hodinhull, Warwickshire, England, and was connected with the family of Lord Charles How, Earl of Lancaster, during the reign of Charles I. The grandfather, who perhaps first resided at Watertown, was admitted a freeman of Sudbury on May 13th, 1640, and in 1642 was marshal and one of the town's selectmen. In May, 1656, he was one of thirteen petitioners for the grant which constituted Marlborough, and moved to that place in 1657, where he opened the first tavern about 1661, and was certainly carrying on the business in 1670. He built himself a cabin in Marlborough "a little to the east of the Indian Planting Field," where his descendants lived for many generations. John How was a leading citizen of the place, and died there on May 28th, 1687, his

---

*These genealogical data are interpreted from conflicting statements in Hudson's *History of Sudbury, Mass.*, pp. 38-39; *Vital Records of Sudbury, Mass.*, (1903), pp. 73-74, 219-220, 311-312; Hudson's *History of Marlborough, Mass.*, pp. 380-381; Pierce's *History of Grafton, Mass.*, pp. 51, 59, 507-508; Temple and Sheldon's *History of Northfield, Mass.*, pp. 468-469; *Worcester Magazine*, vol. ii (1826), p. 131; *Memorial of the Morses*, Boston, 1850, appendix, p. 87, No. 12; and chapter on "Howe Family in America," in *Filial Tribute to Memory of Rev. John Moffat Howe*, pp. 8, 9, 11.

will being proved in 1689. By his wife, Mary, he had ten sons and two daughters, born between 1641 and 1663.

One of his sons, Samuel, father of Nehemiah, was born in Sudbury, on October 20th, 1642. His first wife was Martha Bent, whom he married in Sudbury on June 5th, 1663. She died on August 29th, 1680. They had a numerous issue. His second consort was the widow Sarah (Leavitt) Clapp, whom he married in Sudbury, on September 18th, 1685. Lieut. Samuel How died at Sudbury, on April 13th, 1713.

Nehemiah How was apparently the third child by the second marriage, and was born in 1693 at Marlborough (there is no entry of his birth in the printed Sudbury vital records). He was in Sudbury in 1716; removed to Grafton in 1728, where he received a partition of five acres of land, on May 21st, 1733. The record shows him an active participant at the meetings of the proprietors of Grafton, and they sometimes met at his house. In 1734, he was moderator at two meetings of this body, was selectman in 1735; town clerk from 1736-1738; assessor in 1737; on the school committee of Grafton in 1739, and constable in that year. About that year he removed to the Great Meadow, as one of the original settlers there. Nehemiah married Margaret, the daughter of Capt. Benjamin Willard, and they had twelve children, as follows:

1. Joshua, b. October 11th, 1716; m. Lydia Robbins.
2. Submit, b. March 4th, 1718.
3. Caleb, b. January 30th, 1720; d. June 2d, 1721.
4. Easter, b. April 25th, 1722.
5. Caleb, b. December 31st, 1723; m. Jemima, widow of William Phips. She suffered a doleful captivity in 1755, and he was scalped and died on July 28th, 1755, in the same incursion.
6. Sarah, b. July 13th, 1725.
7. Samuel, b. June 15th, 1727.
8. Edward, b. May 28th, 1728.
9. Abner, b. October 20th, 1731.
10. Hannah, b. November 29th, 1733.
11. Mary, b. April 12th, 1735.
12. Martha, b. September 16th, 1738.

The capture and imprisonment of Nehemiah How are treated fully in the "Introduction" to this volume. While in prison at Quebec, Canada, he became ill "of ye Fever,"* about the middle of the month of May, 1747, and was removed to "the Hospital," where he died on the 25th of that month, after an incarceration of "one Year, seven Months, and fifteen Days."† In a postscript to his printed tract some anonymous friend added this tribute: "He was a loving Husband, and a tender Father; greatly belov'd by his Brethren and

---
*Pote's *Journal*, p. 135.
†How, p. 22.

Sisters, and indeed by every One who was acquainted with him: Mr. How was a Person who had behav'd himself as a Christian from his Youth. His Death is a great Loss to his Friends; but I believe a Gain to himself; and that he is gone from a Captivity of Sorrow on Earth, to join in Songs of everlasting Joy among the Ransom'd of the Lord in the heavenly Zion."* His fellow prisoner, Pote, recorded in his journal that How was "a Good Pious old Gentleman . . . and ye most Contented and Easey of any man In ye Prison."†

VICTOR HUGO PALTSITS.

New York, January 9th, 1904.

---

*How, p. 22.
†Pote, p. 135.

HOW'S NARRATIVE
BOSTON, 1748

*Reprinted from a copy of the original edition
in the New York Public Library
(Lenox Building)*

A NARRATIVE Of the Captivity OF 𝕹𝖊𝖍𝖊𝖒𝖎𝖆𝖍 𝕳𝖔𝖜,

Who was taken by the **Indians** at the *Great-Meadow Fort* above *Fort-Dummer*, where he was an Inhabitant, *October* 11th 1745.

Giving an Account of what he met with in his travelling to *Canada*, and while he was in Prison there.

Together with an Account of Mr. HOW's Death at *Canada*.

Pſal. cxxxvii. 1,2,3,4. *By the Rivers of Babylon, there we sat down ---We hanged our Harps upon the Willows, in the midst thereof. For there they that carried us away captive, required of us a Song; and they that wasted us, required of us Mirth, saying, Sing us one of the Songs of Zion. How shall we sing the Lord's Song in a strange Land.*

BOSTON: N.E.
Printed and Sold opposite to the Prison in Queen-Street. 1748.

[3] HOW'S NARRATIVE &c.

AT the *Great - Meadow - Fort** fourteen Miles above *Fort-Dummer, October* 11th 1745, where I was an Inhabitant, I went out from the Fort about 50 Rods to cut Wood; and when I had done, I walk'd towards the Fort, but in my Way heard the crackling of Fences behind me, & turning about, faw 12 or 13 Indians, with red painted Heads, running after me: On which I cry'd to God for Help, and ran, and hollow'd as I ran, to alarm the Fort; but by that I had ran ten Rods, the Indians came up with me and took hold of me: At the fame Time the Men at the Fort fhot at the Indians, and kill'd one on the Spot, wounded another, who died fourteen Days after he got Home, and likewife fhot a Bullet thro' the Powder-Horn of one that had hold of me. They then led me into the Swamp† and pinion'd me. I then committed my Cafe to God, and Pray'd, that fince it was his Will to deliver me into the Hands of thefe cruel Men, I might find Favour in their Eyes: Which

---

*Now Putney, Windham County, Vt. The history of this incursion is given *in extenso*, in the Introduction to this volume.

†Probably where the creek now is.—David L. Mansfield, in Hemenway's *Gazetteer*, vol. v, p. 252.

Requeſt, God of his infinite Mercy was pleaſed to grant; for they were generally kind to me while I was with 'em: Some of the Indians, at that Time, took the Charge of [4] me, others ran into the Field to kill Cattle. They led me about half a Mile; where we ſtaid in open Sight of the Fort, 'till the Indians who were killing Cattle came to us laden with Beef: Then they went a little further to a Houſe, where they ſtay'd to cut the Meat from the Bones, and cut the Helve off my Ax, and ſtuck it into the Ground, pointing the Way we went.

Then we travel'd along by the River Side;* and when we got about three Miles, I eſpied a Canoe coming down on the further Side the River, with *David Rugg* and *Robert Baker* belonging to our Fort. I made as much Noiſe as I could, by Hamming &c. that they might ſee us before the Indians ſaw them, and ſo get aſhore, and happily eſcape; but the Indians ſaw them, and ſhot a-croſs the River twenty or thirty Guns at them, and kill'd the firſt mention'd Perſon, viz. *David Rugg*, but *Robert Baker* the other Perſon got aſhore, and eſcaped. Then ſome of the Indians ſwam over the River, & bro't the Canoe over the River, ſcalp'd & ſtript the dead Man, and then went about a Mile further, when we came to another Houſe, where we ſtop'd; while there, we heard Men running by the Bank of the River, whom I knew to be *Jonathan Thay-*

---
*Connecticut River.

er, *Samuel Nutting*, & my Son *Caleb How*: Five of the Indians ran to head them. My Heart ak'd for them, & pray'd to God to fave them from the Hands of the Enemy. I fuppofe they hid under the Bank of the River; for the Indians were gone fome Time, but came back without them, bleffed be God.

We went about a Mile further, where we lodg'd that Night, and roafted the Meat they had got: The next Day we travel'd very flow, by Reafon of the In- [5] dian who was wounded, which was a great Favour to me. We lodg'd the fecond Night againft Number *Four*;* the third Day we likewife travel'd flowly, and ftop'd often to reft, & to get along the wounded Man; we lodg'd that Night by the fecond fmall River† that runs into the great River againft Numb. *Four*.

The fourth Day Morning, the Indians held a Piece of Bark, and bid me write my Name, & how many Days we had travel'd; for, faid they, *May be Englifh-Men will come here*. That was a hard Day to me; for it was a wet Day, and we went over prodigious Mountains, fo that I became weak & faint; for I had not eaten the value of one Meal from the Time I was taken, having nothing to eat but Beef

---

*Now Charlestown, N. H., so called in honor of Sir Charles Knowles. In 1745 it was the most northern settlement on the Connecticut River.

†Black River, located on the Morris Map, 1749, published with William Pote's *Journal*; also on Sauthier's map of New York, 1779.

almoſt raw, without Bread or Salt. When I came firſt to the Foot of thoſe Hills, I tho't it was impoſſible for me to aſcend them, without immediate Help from God; therefore my conſtant Recourſe was to him for Strength; which he was gracioufly pleaſed to grant me; and for which I deſire to Praiſe him. We got that Day a little before Night to a Place where they had a hunting Houſe, a Kettle, ſome Beef,* Indian Corn, and Salt: They boil'd a good Meſs of it; I drank of the Broth, eat of the Meat & Corn, and was wonderfully refreſhed, ſo that I felt like another Man.

The next Morning we got up early, and after we had eaten, my Maſter ſaid to me, *You muſt quick walk to Day, or I will kill you.* I told him I would go as faſt as I could, and no faſter, if he did kill me: At which, an old Indian who was the beſt Friend I had, took Care of me. We travel'd that Day very hard, and over ſteep Hills, but it being a cool windy [6] Day, I perform'd it with more Eaſe than before; yet I was much tired before Night, but dare not complain.

The next Day the Indians gave me a Pair of their Shoes, ſo that I travel'd with abundant more Eaſe than when I wore my own Shoes; tho' I eat but very little, our Victuals being almoſt ſpent; when the Sun was about two Hours high, the Indians ſcattered to hunt, and

---

*Misprinted "Beer" in the original, but corrected by a contemporary hand in the copy used for this reprint.

they foon kill'd a Fawn, & three fmall Bears; fo that we had again Meat enough, fome of which we boil'd, and eat heartily of, by which I felt ftrong.

The next Day we travel'd very hard, and perform'd it with Eafe; infomuch that one of the Indians told me, I was a very ftrong Man: About three of the Clock we came to the Lake,* where they had five Canoes, and Pork, Indian Corn, & Tobacco. We got into the Canoes, when the Indians ftuck up a Pole about eight Feet long with the Scalp of *David Rugg* on the Top of it, painted red, with the Likenefs of Eyes and Mouth on it: We fail'd about ten Miles, and then went on Shore; and after we had made a Fire, we boil'd a good Supper, and eat heartily.

The next Day we fet fail for *Crown-Point*, but when we were within a Mile of the Place, they went on Shore, where were eight or ten French & Indians, but before I got on Shore two of them came running into the Water Knee deep, and pull'd me out of the Canoe; there they fang and danced round me, after which one of them bid me fet down, which I did; and then they pull'd off my Shoes and Buckles, and [7] took them from me. Soon after we went along to *Crown-Point*, and when we got there, the People both French and Indians were very thick by the Water-Side;

---

*Probably they embarked nearly opposite Ticonderoga, at about the present Larrabee's Point.

two of the Indians took me out of the Canoe, and leading me, bid me run, which we did; it was about twenty Rods from the Fort; the Fort is large, built with Stone & Lime; they led me up to the third Loft, where was the Captain's Chamber; a Chair was bro't that I might fet by the Fire and warm me. Soon after the Indians that I belong'd to, and others that were there, came into the Chamber, among whom was one I knew, named *Pealtomy*; he came and fpake to me, and fhook Hands with me; and I was glad to fee him: He went out, but foon return'd and brought to me another Indian named *Amrufus*,* Hufband to Mrs. *Eunice Williams*, Daughter of the late Rev. Mr. *Williams*† of *Deerfield*; he was glad to fee me, and I to fee him. He afked me after his Wife's Relations, and

---

*Eunice Williams, born on September 16th, 1696, daughter of Rev. John Williams. of Deerfield, Mass., was carried captive to Canada in 1704. She remained there and married an Indian, assumed Indian habits, and forgot what English she had known. In Canada she died at the age of about ninety years. The Rev. Eleazer Williams, her great-grandson, stated that she married an Indian by the name of De Rogers, but I believe How is nearer the truth, since De Rogers may have been phonetically misunderstood for Amrusus.—*Williams Genealogy.* Greenfield, 1847, pp. 92, ff.

†Rev. John Williams, first minister of Deerfield, was captured there by French and Indians on February 29th, 1703-4. He was carried into captivity to Canada; was redeemed, and left Quebec on October 25th, 1706, for Boston, where he arrived on November 21st. He published an account of his captivity, namely, *The Redeemed Captive, Returning to Zion.* Boston: B. Green, 1707. A second edition was printed during his lifetime, and there have been many editions since.

shew'd a great deal of Respect to me. A while after this, the Indians sat in a Ring in the Chamber, and *Pealtomy* came to me, and told me, I must go sing and dance before the Indians; I told him, I could not: He told me over some Indian Words, and bid me sing *them*: I told him, I could not. With that the rest of the Fort who could speak some English came to me, & bid me sing it in English, which was, *I don't know where I go*; which I did, dancing round that Ring three Times; and then I sat down by the Fire: The Priest came to me, and gave me a Dram of Rum; after that the Captain brought me Part of a Loaf of Bread and a Plate of Butter, and ask'd me [8] to eat, which I did heartily; for I had not eaten any Bread from the Time I was taken till then. The French Priest and all the Officers shew'd me a great deal of Respect: The Captain gave me a Pair of good Buckskin Shoes, the Priest fix'd them on my Feet; and we stay'd there that Night; where I slept with the Priest, Captain & Lieut: The Lieutenant's Name was *Ballock*,* he had been a Prisoner at *Boston*, and had been at *Northampton* and the Towns thereabouts. This Day, which was the Sabbath, I was well treated by the French Officers with Victuals and Drink: We tarried there 'till Noon, then went off about a Mile, and put on

---

*No doubt this refers to Sieur de Beaulac, "a reformed lieutenant," who commanded at Fort Chambly in 1746.—*N. Y. Col. Docs.*, vol. x, p. 36.

Shore; where they ſtay'd the reſt of the Day, and having Rum with them, moſt of them were much Liquor'd. *Pealtomy* and his Squaw, and another Indian Family went with us, and by them I found out that *Wm. Phips** kill'd an Indian, beſides that we† wounded before he was kill'd, for an Indian who was with us, aſk'd me, if there was one kill'd near our Fort laſt Summer? I told him, I did not know: He ſaid he had a Brother went out then, and had not ſeen him ſince, and that he had heard he was kill'd at our Fort, and wanted to know if it was true: But I did not think it beſt to tell him any ſuch Thing was ſuſpected.

But the Indians now got into a Frolick and quarel'd about me; they made me ſet in the Canoe by the Water-ſide: I was afraid they would hurt if not kill me: They attempted to come to me, but the ſober Indians hinder'd them that were in Liquor. *Pealtomy* ſeeing the Rout went to the Fort, and ſoon after Lieut. *Ballock*, with ſome Soldiers, came to us, [9] and when the Indians were made eaſy, they went away: We lodg'd there that Night, and the next Day was a ſtormy Day of Wind

---

*William Phips was one of the original settlers of the Great Meadow (Putney, Vt.). He was captured by the Indians on July 5th, 1745, while hoeing in his corn-field at the south-west corner of the meadow, and he was butchered about a half mile from the place, but not without his first succeeding in killing one of his captors and mortally wounding another.—*Cf.* Doolittle's *Short Narrative*. Boston, 1750, p. 2; *N. E. Hist. and Gen. Register*, vol. ix, p. 163.

†A misprint in the original for "he."

Snow & Rain; ſo that we* forc'd to tarry there that Day and the next Night; in this Time the Indians continued fetching Rum from the Fort, and kept half drunk: Here I underwent ſome Hardſhip by ſtaying there ſo long in a Storm without Shelter or Blanket. They had a great Dance that Night, and hung up *David Rugg's* Scalp on a Pole, dancing round it: After they had done, they lay down to ſleep.

The next Morning, which was the tenth Day from the Time of my being taken, we went off in a Canoe, and the Night after we arriv'd at the wide *Lake*,† and there we stay'd that Night; ſome of the Indians went a hunting, and kill'd a fat Buck-Deer, ſo that we had Victuals plenty, for we had a full Supply of Bread given us at the Fort at *Crown-Point*.

The next Morning the Wind being calm, we ſet out about two Hours before Day; ſoon after came to a Schooner lying at Anchor, went on Board, the French treated us very civilly: They gave each of us a Dram of Rum, and Victuals to eat. As ſoon as it was Day we left the Schooner, & two Hours before Sun-ſet got over the Lake, & next Day came to *Shamballee*,‡ where we met 300 French and 200 Indians, who did the Miſchief at &

---

*The omission of "were" is so in the original.
†Lake Champlain.
‡Fort Chambly, named from Jacques de Chambly, founder of the seigniory of Chambly. How's form is merely one of several phonetical spellings which are numerous in the documents.

about Mr. *Lydius*'s Fort.* I was taken out of the Canoe by two Frenchmen, and fled to a Houſe about ten Rods off as faſt as I could run, the Indians flinging Snow-Balls at me. As ſoon as I got to the Houſe, the Indians ſtood round me very thick, and bid me ſing & dance; which I did with [10] them, in their Way, then they gave a Shout, and left off. Two of them came to me, one of whom ſmote me on one Cheek, to'ther† on the other, which made the Blood run plentifully. Then they bid me ſing and dance again, which I did with them, and they with me, ſhouting as before. Then two French Men took me under each Arm, and run ſo faſt that the Indians could not keep up with us to hurt me: We ran about 40 Rods to another Houſe; where a Chair was bro't for me to ſet down: The Houſe was ſoon full of French & Indians, and round the Houſe they were looking in at the Windows. A French Gentleman came to me, took me by the Hand, and led me into a ſmall Room, where none came in but ſuch as he admitted: He gave me Victuals and Drink: Several French Gentlemen and Indians came in, and were civil to me. The Indians who came in, could ſpeak Engliſh; they ſhook Hands with me, call'd me, Brother. They told me they were all Soldiers, and were going to *New-*

---

*Fort Edward, often called Fort Lydius, after John Henry Lydius, who was governor there for many years.
†A vagary for "t'other."

England: They faid, they fhould go to my Town; which was a great Damp to my Spirit, 'till I heard of their Return, where they had been, and what they had done. A while after this, the Indians whom I belong'd to, came to me, and told me we muft go; which we did; and after going down the River about two Miles, we came to the thickeft of the Town, where was a large Fort built with Stone and Lime, & very large and fine Houfes in it; where was the General of the Army I fpake of before: He afked me, what News from *London* and *Bofton*; I told him fuch as I tho't convenient, and omitted the reft; and then [11] went down to the Canoes, when fome of the Indians went and got a plenty of Bread & Beef, which they put into the Canoes, and then we went into a French Houfe, where we had a good Supper: There came in feveral French Gentlemen to fee me, who were civil to me; one of them gave me a *Crown* Sterl. We lodg'd there 'till about two Hours before Day, when we arofe, and went down the River;* I fuppofe we went a Hundred Miles† that Day, which bro't us into the great River call'd *Quebec-River*; we lodg'd that Night in a French Houfe, and were civilly treated.

The next Day we went down the River, and I was carried before the Governour there,

---

*The Sorel River, also called Richelieu and Chambly.
†Evidently an exaggeration, unless the distance included the Sorel and part of the St. Lawrence.

which was the Sabbath, and the 16th Day after my being taken. We ſtay'd there about three Hours, and were well treated by the French; and then the Indians were order'd to carry me down to *Quebeck*; which was 90 Miles further: We went down the River about three Miles that Night; then went aſhore, and lodg'd the remainder of the Night.

The next Morning we ſet off, and the ſecond Day which was the 18th from the Time I was taken, we arrived at *Quebec*. The Land is inhabited on both Sides the River from the Lake to *Quebec*, which is at leaſt two Hundred Miles, but eſpecially from *Shamballe* very thick, ſo that the Houſes are within Sight of one another all the Way.

But to return; after we arrived at *Quebec,* I was carried up into a large Chamber which was full of Indians, who were civil to me: Many of the French came in to ſee me, and were very kind to me: I [12] ſtay'd there about two Hours, when a French Gentleman who could ſpeak good Engliſh came in and told me, I muſt go with him to the Governour; which I did; and after anſwering to a great many Queſtions,* and treated with as much Bread & Wine as I deſired, I was ſent with an Officer to the Guard Houſe, and led into a ſmall Room, where was an Engliſh-Man

---

*The nature of the questions and How's replies are given in *Collection de Manuscrits relatifs à la Nouvelle-France*, vol. iii, pp. 268-270.

named *William Stroud,* a Kinſman of the Hon. Judge *Lynde's* in *New-England*: He belong'd to *South-Carolina,* and had been at *Quebec* ſix Years, whom the Governour kept confin'd for fear he ſhou'd leave them and go to *New-England,* and diſcover their Strength: Mr. *Stroud* and I were kept in the Guard-Houſe one Week, with a Sufficiency of Food and Drink: The French Gentlemen kept coming in to ſee me, & was very civilly treated by them: I had the better Opportunity of diſcourſing with them as Mr. *Stroud* was a good Interpreter.

After this we were ſent to Priſon, where I found one *James Kinlade,** who was taken 14 Days before I was, at *Sheepſcot* at the Eaſtward in *New-England*: I was much pleaſed with his Converſation, eſteeming him a Man of true Piety: We were kept in Priſon eight Days, with Liberty to keep in the Room with the Priſon-keeper. We were daily viſited by Gentlemen and Ladies, who ſhew'd us great Kindneſs, in giving us Money and other Things, and a pleaſant Behaviour towards us; bleſſed be God therefor, for I deſire to aſcribe all the Favours I have been the Partaker of ever ſince my Captivity, to the abundant

---

*Kincaid, Kinkead or Kinkhead is of Gaelic origin, and in Scotland is written Kincade. He was captured on September 27th, 1745. His deposition to the French is printed in *Coll. de MSS. relatifs à la N.-F.*, vol. iii, pp. 261-262.

Grace & Goodnefs of a bountiful God, as the firft Caufe.

[13] After this, Mr. *Kinlade* and I were fend* to another Prifon, where were 22 Seamen belonging to feveral Parts of our King's Dominions, three of them Captains of Veffels, viz *James Southerland*† of *Cape-Cod*, *William Chipman*‡ of *Marblehead*, *William Pote*§ of *Cafco-Bay*; this Prifon was a large House built with Stone & Lime two Feet thick, and about 120 Feet long. We had two large Stoves in it, & Wood enough, fo that we could keep ourfelves warm in the coldeft Weather. We had Provifion fufficient, viz. two Pound of good Wheat Bread, one Pound of Beef, and Peas anfwerable, to each Man ready drefs'd every day.‖

When I had been there a few Days the Captives defir'd me to lead them in carrying

---

*So printed in the original.

†James Sutherland, commander of the schooner *Seaflower*. He was captured in Annapolis Basin, Nova Scotia, with Captain William Pote, Jr., and the full details are recorded in the *Journal* of the latter.

‡William Chapman was captured with his brigantine while "Bound from Maryland to London," on May 24th, 1745.—Pote's *Journal*, p. 80.

§His personal history is given in the appendix to his newly-found journal, edited by me for Bishop John F. Hurst.—*The Journal of Captain William Pote, Jr., during his Captivity in the French and Indian War from May, 1745, to August, 1747.* New York: Dodd, Mead & Company, 1896. 8vo, pp. xxxvii+223, with Charles Morris's map of 1749. In this work I have recorded the personal history of nearly all the captives referred to in How's pamphlet.

‖How was brought to this prison on Sunday, November 17th, 1745.

on Morning and Evening Devotion, which I was willing to do: We had a Bible, a Pſalm-Book, and ſome other good Books; our conſtant Practice was to read a Chapter in the Bible, and ſing Part of a Pſalm, and to pray, Night and Morning.

When I was at the firſt Priſon I was ſtript of all my old and louſey Cloaths, and had other Cloathing given me from Head to Foot, and had many Kindneſſes ſhewn me by thoſe that liv'd thereabouts, more eſpecially by one Mr. *Corby* and his Wife, who gave me Money there, and brought me many good Things at the other Priſon. But here I was taken ill, as was alſo moſt of the other Priſoners, with a Flux, which laſted near a Month, ſo that I was grown very weak, but after that I was healthful, thro' divine Goodneſs, bleſſed be God for it: I was much concern'd for my Country, eſpecially for the Place I was taken from, [14] by Reaſon that I met an Army going thither, as they told me: The 27th Day of *November** we had News come to the Priſon that they were come back to *Shamballe,* and had taken upwards of a Hundred Captives, which increas'd my Concern, for I expected our Fort, & others thereabouts, were deſtroy'd, which put me upon earneſt Prayer to God, that he would give me Grace to ſubmit

---

*This information supplies a partial gap in Pote's *Journal.* It refers to the attack on Saratoga, the present Schuylerville, on the night of November 28 and 29 (new style), 1745.

to his Will; after which I was eafy in my Mind.

About a Fortnight after,* a Dutchman was bro't to Prifon, who was one of the Captives the faid Army had taken; he told me they had burnt Mr. *Lydius's* Fort, and all the Houfes at that new Townfhip, and had kill'd Capt. *Schyler*† and five or fix more, and had brought 50 Whites and about 60 Negroes to *Montreal*: I was forry to hear of fo much Mifchief done, but rejoyc'd they had not been upon our River and the Towns thereabouts; for which I gave Thanks to God for his great Goodnefs in preferving them, and particularly my Family.

When Chriftmas came,‡ the Governour fent us 24 Livres; the Lord-Intendant came into the Prifon and gave us 24 Livres more, which was about two Guineas: He told us he hop'd we fhould be fent Home in a little Time; he was a pleafant Gentleman, and very kind to the Captives: Some time after Mr. *Shearly*§ a Gentleman of Quality came to us, and gave to the three Sea Captains 24 Livres, and to me twelve, and the next Day fent me a Bottle of Claret Wine. About ten Days after he fent

---

*December 11th (old style).—Pote, p. 85.

†Apparently Capt. Nicholas Schuyler is meant, but he was not killed.

‡The Canadians of course celebrated Christmas eleven days earlier than the New Englanders, or according to "new style."—*Cf.* Pote, p. 85, under date of December 15th.

§M. de Chalet, interpreter of the King. This visit was made on January 10th, 1745-6.—*Cf.* Pote, p. 85.

me twelve Livres more; it was in all *eight Pounds* old Tenor.

[15] *January* 20th 1745, 6. Eighteen Captives* were brought from *Montreal* to the Prifon at *Quebec*, which is 180 Miles.

February 22. Seven Captives more who were taken at *Albany*† were brought to the Prifon to us, *viz*. fix Men and one old Woman 70 Years old, who had been fo infirm for feven Years paft, fhe had not been able to walk the Streets, yet perform'd this tedious Journey with Eafe.

March 15. One of the Captives taken at *Albany* after 14 or 15 Days Sicknefs died in the Hofpital at *Quebec*, a Man of a fober pious Converfation, his Name was *Lawrence Plaffer*,‡ a German born.

May 3d 1746. Three Captives taken at Number *Four*, fixteen Miles above where I was taken, *viz*. Capt. *John Spafford, Ifaac Parker,* and *Stephen Farnfworth,* were brought to Prifon to us; who inform'd me my Family was well a few Days before they were taken, which rejoyc'd me much. I was forry for the Misfortune of thefe my Friends, but was glad of their Company, and of their

---

*They were among those whom Lieutenant Marin had taken captive at Saratoga.—Pote, p. 86.

†Saratoga is correct.

‡During the many months in which captives had been confined in this prison, none had died. Lawrence **Platter** or Plater, according to Norton, p. 30, and Pote, p. 165, was the first to succumb to illness. He also was captured at Saratoga.

being well ufed by thofe who took them: Let God have the Praife.

May 14. Two Captives were brought into Prifon, *viz. Jacob Read* and *Edward Cloutman*, taken at a new Townfhip called *Gorham-Town* near *Cafco-Bay*. They inform'd us that one Man, and four Children of one of them were kill'd and his Wife taken at the fame Time with them, & was in the Hands of Indians.*

May 16. Two lads, viz. *James* & *Samuel Anderfon*, Brothers, taken at *Sheepfcot* were bro't to Prifon.

May 17. *Samuel Burbank* & *David Woodwell*, who were taken at *New-Hopkington* near *Rumford*, were [16] brought to Prifon, and inform'd us, there were taken with them two Sons of the faid *Burbank*, and the Wife, two Sons and a Daughter of the faid *Woodwell*, whom they left in the Hands of the Indians.†

May 24. *Thomas Jones* of *Hollifton*, who was a Soldier at *Contocook*, was brought to Prifon, and told us, that one *Elifha Cook*, and a Negro belonging to the Rev Mr. *Stevens,* were kill'd, when he was taken.‡

June 1. *William Aikings*§ taken at Pleaf-

---

*William Bryant and family. See names and details in Pote's *Journal*, pp. 88, 97, 104, 117.
†Compare Pote's *Journal*, pp. 89, 90.
‡Fuller details are given in Pote, p. 90.
§William Akins.—Pote, p. 90.

ant Point near *George's Fort* was brought alſo to Priſon.

June 2. Mr *Shearly** brought ſeveral Letters of Deacon *Timothy Brown*'s of *Lower-Aſhuelots*,† and Money, and deliver'd them to me; which made us think he was kill'd or taken. A few Days after, Mr. *Shearly* told me he was taken: I was glad to hear he was alive.

June 6. *Timothy Cumings*‡ aged 60 was bro't to Priſon, who inform'd us, he was at Work with five other Men, about 40 Rods from the Block-Houſe at *George*'s, when five Indians ſhot at them, but hurt none. The Men ran away and left him & their Guns to the Indians; he told us that the Enſign was kill'd as he ſtood on the Top of the Fort, and that the Engliſh kill'd five Indians at the ſame Time.

June 13. Mr. *Shearly* bro't to the Captives ſome Letters which were ſent from *Albany,* and among them one from Lieut Governour *Phipps* of the *Maſſachuſetts-Bay*, to the Governour of *Canada*, for the Exchange of Priſoners, which gave us great Hopes of a ſpeedy Releaſe.

June 22. Eight Men were brought to Priſon, among whom was Deacon *Brown* and

---
*De Chalet.
†Now Swanzey, N. H.
‡Timothy Cummings.

Robert Morfe,* [17] who inform me there was fix or eight Indians kill'd a little before they were taken at *Upper-Afhuelots*, and that they learnt by the Indians who took them, there were fix more of the Englifh kill'd at other Places near *Connecticut-River*; & feveral more much wounded; thefe laft, were fuppos'd to be the Wife and Children of the aforefaid *Burbank* and *Woodwell*.

July 5. We fent a Petition to the chief Governor that we might be exchang'd; and the 7th Mr. *Shearly* told us we fhould be exchang'd for other Captives in a little Time; which caus'd great Joy among us: The fame Day at Night *John Beman* of *Northfield* was bro't to Prifon, who told us, that an Expedition againft *Canada* was on Foot, which much rejoyc'd us: He alfo told us of the three Fights at Number *Four*, and who were kill'd & taken; and of Mifchief done in feveral other Places near *Connecticut-River*; and that my Brother *Daniel How's* Son *Daniel* was taken with him, and was in the Hands of Indians, who defsign'd to keep him.†

July 20. *John Jones* a Seaman was brought into Prifon, who told us he was going from

---

*Deacon Timothy Brown and Robert Moffat.—Pote, p. 91.

†John Beaumont, Beaman or Bement and Daniel How were captured during an attack upon a number of men at work in the meadow at Bridgman's fort, on the site of Vernon, Vermont.—*Cf.* Pote, pp. 91, 92.

Cape-Breton to *Newfoundland* with one Engliſhman, and four Frenchmen who had ſworn Allegiance to King George, and in the Paſſage kill'd the other Engliſhman, but carried *him* to the Bay of *Arb*, where there was an Army of French and Indians, to whom they deliver'd him; and by them was ſent to *Quebec*.

July 21. *John Richards* and a Boy of nine or ten Years old, who belong'd to *Rocheſter* in *New-Hampſhire*, were brought to Priſon, and told us, there were four Engliſhmen kill'd when they were taken.*

[18] *Auguſt* 15. Seven Captives, who with eight more taken at *St. John*'s *Iſland*, were bro't to Priſon, and told us, that ſeveral were kill'd after Quarters were given, among whom was *James Owen* late of *Brookfield* in *New-England.*†

Auguſt 16. *Thomas Jones* late of *Sherburne* in *New-England*, after 7 or 8 Days Sickneſs died: He gave good Satisfaction as to his future State.

Auguſt 25. We had at *Canada* a Squal of Snow.

September 12. *Robert Downing*‡ who had been a Soldier at *Cape-Breton*, and was taken at *St. John*'s, and who was with the Indians

---

*For a full account see Pote, p. 93.
†For their names and the circumstances of their capture, see Pote, p. 93.
‡Pote calls him "Robt· Dewen."

two Months, and fuffer'd great Abufe from them, was brought to Prifon.

September 15. Twenty-three of the Captives taken at *Hoofuck-Fort** were brought to Prifon, among whom was the Reverend Mr. *John Norton*: They inform us, that after fighting 26 Hours with 800 French and Indians, they furrendered themfelves on Capitulation Prifoners of War: They alfo inform'd us, that *Thomas Nalton*† and *Jofiah Read*‡ were kill'd when they were taken. The Names of thofe now brought in Prifoners, are as follows, *viz.* The Rev. Mr. *John Norton, John Hawks, John Smeed,* his Wife and fix Children, *John Perry* and his Wife, *Mofes Scot* his Wife and two Children, *Samuel Goodman, Jonathan Bridgman, Nathan Emes,*§ *Jofeph Scot, Amos Pratt, Benjamin Sinconds, Samuel Lovet, David Warren,* and *Phineas Furbufh*:‖

---

*Fort Massachusetts, in the present town of Adams, Berkshire County, Mass. The best contemporary account of its surrender is contained in Rev. John Norton's *The Redeemed Captive, Being a Narrative Of the taking and carrying into Captivity The Reverend Mr. John Norton When Fort Massachusetts Surrendered to a large Body of French and Indians Aug. 20th, 1746.* Boston, 1748. It was reprinted by Samuel G. Drake in 1870.

†Thomas Knowlton was shot through the head on the morning of August 20th, before the fort surrendered, "so that some of his brains came out, yet life remained in him for some hours."—Norton, p. 8.

‡Josiah Reed had a "long and tedious sickness" at the time of the surrender, and "either died of his illness, or else was killed by the enemy," on the following night.—Norton, pp. 12, 14.

§Nathan Eames.

‖Phinehas Forbush.

The two laſt of theſe inform me, that my Brother *Daniel How's* Son was taken from the Indians, and lives with a French Gentleman at *Montreal*. There were four Captives more taken at *Albany* the laſt Summer brought to Priſon the ſame Day.*

[19] *September* 26. Seventy-four Men and two Women taken at Sea were brought to Priſon.†

October 1. *Jacob Shepard*‡ of *Weſtborough*, taken at *Hooſuck*, was brought to Priſon.

Octob. 3. *Jonath. Batherick*§ was bro't to Priſon.

October 5. Seventeen Men were brought to Priſon, three of them taken with Mr. *Norton* & others, viz. *Nath. Hitchcock, John Aldrick*,‖ and *Stephen Scot*: *Richard Subes*¶ who was taken at *New-Caſco*, ſays, one Man was kill'd at the ſame Time: Alſo *Pike*

---

 *Pote records the advent of the four from Albany, under date of September 24th.

 †They were a part of the prisoners captured by the French vessels, *Le Castor* and *L'Aurore*.—Pote's *Journal*, pp. 96-97.

 ‡Jacob Shepherd was captured at Fort Massachusetts; was "a pious young man, well beloved," and died in captivity on May 30th, 1747.—Pote, pp. 98, 136; Norton, p. 39.

 §This is an error. His name was Jonathan Donham or Dunham, a soldier, captured with Pote on May 17th, 1745. He died on November 28th, 1746, after an illness of eight or ten days, of inflammation of the lungs.—Pote, p. 98.

 ‖John Aldrich.—Norton, p. 29.

 ¶Richard Stubs, who was captured August 26th, 1746.—Pote, p. 98.

Gooden* taken at *Saco*, was bro't to Prifon; he alfo fays, he had a Brother kill'd at the fame Time.

October 12. 24 Seamen were bro't to Prifon.†

October 19. Six Seamen were brought to Prifon.‡

October 20. *Jacob Read* died.

October 23. *Edward Cloutman* and *Robert Dunbar* broke Prifon, and went for *New-England*.

October 27. A Man was brought to Prifon, and fays, the Indians took five more, and brought ten Scalps to *Montreal*.

Nov. 1. *John Read* died.

Nov. 9. *John Davis* taken with Mr. *Norman* died.

Nov. 17. *Nathan Eames* of *Marlborough* died.

Nov. 19. Mr. *Adams*§ taken at *Sheepfcot* was bro't to Prifon, and fays that *James Anderfon*'s Father was kill'd, and his Uncle taken at the fame Time.

Nov. 20. *Leonard Lydle* & the Widow *Sarah Briant*, were married in *Canada* by the Reverend Mr. *Norton*.

---

*Pike Gordon, son of Joseph Gordon, of Saco.—Pote, p. 106.

†They were another installment of prisoners captured by the vessels *Le Castor* and *L'Aurore*.

‡These belonged to the same as in preceding note.

§Robert Adams.—Pote, p. 103; Norton, p. 32.

Nov. 22. The above ſaid *Anderſon's* Uncle was brought to Priſon.*

Nov. 24. John *Bradſhaw*, who had not been well for moſt of the Time he had been a Priſoner died.

[20] It is a very melancholy Time with us; there are now thirty ſick, and Deaths among us daily.

Nov. 28. *Jonathan Dunham* died.

Nov. 29. Capt. *Bailey*† of *Almſbury* died.

Dec. 1. An *Albany* Man‡ died.

Dec. 6. *Pike Gooden*§ died, and we have Reaſon to think he made a happy Change.

Dec. 7. A Girl‖ of ten Year's of Age died.

Dec. 11. *Moſes Scot's* Wife¶ died.

Dec. 15. One of Capt. *Roberſon's* Lieutenants died.**

Dec. 18. *Daniel Woodwell's* Wife died;†† ſhe was eſteem'd a pious Woman, and we believe made a happy Change.

---

*Capt. John McNear.—Pote, pp. 101, 104.

†Capt. William Bagley is undoubtedly the correct name.—Pote, p. 105; Norton, p. 33.

‡Geret Vanderverick.—Pote, pp. 105, 165. *Cf.* also Norton, p. 33.

§Pike Gordon.

‖Martha Quackinbush.—Pote, p. 106; Norton, p. 33.

¶Miriam Scott.

**John Boon, who belonged to Devonshire, England. He was an "apprentice" to Capt. David Roberts, captured at sea, May 1st, 1746, by *L'Aurore* and *Le Castor.*—Pote, p. 107; Norton, p. 33.

††Mary, wife of David Woodwell, of New Hopkinton.—Pote, pp. 90 (note), 107.

Dec. 23. *John Perry*'s Wife died.*
Dec. 26. *William Dayly*† of *New-York* dy'd hopefully.
Jan. 3. 1746, 7. *Jonathan Harthan*‡ died.
Jan. 4. The Rev. Mr. *Norton* was fo far recover'd from Sicknefs, that he preach'd two Difcourfes from Pfal. 60. 11. *Give us help from Trouble, for vain is the help of Man.*
Jan. 12. Twenty Captives were carried to another Prifon, hoping thereby to cleanfe the other of the Infection; the fame Night one of them died, viz. *Phineas Andrews*§ of *Cape-Ann.*
Jan. 15. *Jacob Bailey* Brother to Capt. *Bailey* aforefaid, died.‖
Jan. 17. *Giat Braban*¶ Capt *Chapman*'s Carpenter died.
Jan. 23. *Samuel Lovet* Son of Major *Lovet* of *Mendon* in *New-England* died.
February 10. *William Garwafs*** died, as did alfo *Mofes Scot's* youngeft Child.††

---

*Rebecah Perry. On November 5th, 1748, John Perry represented his losses at the time of his capture, in a petition to the Bay government, which is preserved in *Mass. Archives*, vol. 73, p. 246.
†Daly, according to Pote, and spelled Daily by Norton.
‡Pote and Norton give his name respectively as Hogadon and Hogadorn.
§Francis Andrews.—Pote, p. 109; Norton, p. 34.
‖Jacob Bagley.
¶Guy Braband.—Pote, p. 110; Guyart Brabbon.—Norton, p. 34.
**"William Galboath, a Scots-man."—Norton, p. 35.
††Also named Moses Scott, and about two years of age. —Norton, p. 35.

Feb. 15. My Nephew *Daniel How* and ſix more [21] were brought down from *Montreal* to *Quebec,* viz. *John Sunderland, John Smith, Richard Smith, William Scot, Philip Scoffil,* and *Benjamin Tainter,* Son to Lieut. *Tainter* of *Weſtborough* in *New-England.*
Febr. 23. *Richard Bennet* died.
Feb. 25. *Michal Dugon** died.
March 18. *James Margra*† died.
March 22. Capt. *John Fort* & *Sam. Goodman* died.
March 28. 1747. The Wife‡ of *John Smeed,* died, who left ſix Children, the youngeſt of which was born the ſecond Night after the Mother was taken.
April 7. *Philip Scaffield* died.
April 8. *John Saneld*§ died.
April 9. Capt. *James Jordan* & one of his Men‖ died.
April 12. *Amos Pratt* of *Shrewſbury* died.
April 14. *Timothy Cummings* died.
April 17. *John Dill* of *Hull*¶ in *New-England* died.

---

*Spelled Dugan by Pote, and Dogan by Norton.

†James Megraw.—Pote, p. 166; "Thomas Magra, an Irishman."—Norton, p. 35.

‡Mary Smeed. For the tragical history of the Smeed or Smead family, see Pote, p. 115 (note).

§John Smeed, son of John Smeed is meant.—Pote, p. 116.

‖Antonio, a Portuguese sailor.—Pote, p. 116; Norton, p. 36.

¶Norton, p. 36, says he "belonged to Nantaskett."

April 18. Samuel Venhon* of *Plimouth* died.

April 26. Capt. *Jonathan Williamſon* was brought to Priſon; he was taken at a new Town on *Sheepſcot River*.

April 26. Three Men were brought to Priſon, who were taken at *Albany* three Weeks before, and tell us, that thirteen were kill'd, Capt. *Trent* one of them, they were all Soldiers for the Expedition to *Canada*.

April 27. *Joſeph Denox*† died.

April 28. *Samuel Evans* died. The ſame Night the Priſon took Fire, and was burnt,‡ but the Things therein were moſtly ſaved: We were kept that Night under a Guard.

May 7. *Sarah Lydle* whoſe Name was *Briant* when ſhe was taken, and married while a Captive, died.

[22] *May* 13. Mr. *Smeed*'s Son *Daniel* died.

May 14. *Chriſtian Fether*§ died. The ſame Day died Mr. *Hezekiah Huntington*, a hopeful Youth of a liberal Education, Son to Col. *Huntington*‖ of *Connecticut*, in New-England.

May 15. *Joſeph Gray* died.

---

*Samuel Vaughan is the correct name.—Pote, p. 118.
†Joseph Denen.—Pote, p. 118; Norton says, "Joseph Denning of Cape Ann."
‡Pote gives a detailed account of the fire.—*Journal*, pp. 122-125.
§Christian Vedder. Pote spells his name "Vader," and Norton gives it as "Tedder."
‖Deacon Hezekiah Huntington, of Norwich, Conn.

May 19. *Samuel Burbanks** died. At the fame Time died two Children† who were put out to the French to Nurfe.

At that Time I received a Letter from Major *Willard*, dated *March* 17. 1747, wherein he informs me, my Family was well; which was joyful News to me.

May 19. *Abraham Fort*‡ died.

---

*Samuel Burbank, of New Hopkinton.
†One of these was Captivity Smeed, aged about nine months. She died, May 17th or 18th.
‡He was a brother of John Fort.

By another Hand.

MAY 25, 1747. This Day died Mr. Nehemiah How, in the Hofpital at *Quebec* in *Canada*, in the 55th Year of his Age; who had been a Captive there one Year, feven Months, and fifteen Days: He enjoy'd his Health 'till about the middle of this Month: He was a loving Hufband, and a tender Father; greatly belov'd by his Brethren and Sifters, and indeed by every One who was acquainted with him: Mr. *How* was a Perfon who had behav'd himfelf as a Chriftian from his Youth. His Death is a great Lofs to his Friends; but I believe a Gain to himfelf; and that he is gone from a Captivity of Sorrow on Earth, to join in Songs of everlafting Joy among the Ranfom'd of the Lord in the heavenly *Zion*.

[23] The Names of the Subfcribers, with the Places of their Abode, to the foregoing Narrative, with the Number of Books fubfcribed for.

Worcester.

The Hon. *John Chandler*, Efq; Six Books.
Major *Daniel Howard*, fix Books.
Mr. *Thomas Wheeler*, fix Books.
Mr. *John Curtifs*, fix Books.
Concord, The Hon. *James Minot*, Efq; fix Books.
Mr. *Thomas Munrow*, fix Books.
Mr. *Henry Flint*, fix Books.
Bofton, Mr. *Jonas Leonard*, fix Books.
Mr. *John Burbeeen* [sic] fix Books.
Rutland, Capt. *Jofeph Stevens*, fix Books.
Capt. *Edward Rice*, fix Books.
Mr. *Mofes Leonard*, fix Books.
Mr. *Andrew Henry*, fix Books.
Mr. *Thomas Flint*, fix Books.
Mr. *Nathan Stone*, fix Books.
Mr. *James Calwell*, fix Books.
Mr. *Jofeph Houlton*, fix Books.
Mr. *Aaron Rofs*, fix Books.
Capt. *John Hubbard*, fix Books.

Rutland,   Mr. *Edward Savage,*   ſix Books.
             Mr. *Eliphalet How,*   ſix Books.
             Mr. *Jonas Stone,*   ſix Books.
             Mr. *Daniel Davis,*   three Books.
             Mr. *Iſrael How,*   ſix Books.
             Mr. *Benjamin Willard,*ſix Books.
             Mr. *Skelten Felton,* ſix Books.
             Deacon *Eleazer Ball,* ſix Books.
             Mr. *Moſes How,*   ſeven Books.
[24] *Lancaſter, Samuel Willard,* Eſq;
                                   ſix Books.
             Mr. *Joſhua Hide,*   ſix Books.
Cambridge, William Brattle, Eſq; ſix Books.
            Edmund Goffe, Eſq;   ſix Books.
Stoughton, John Shepard, Eſq;   ſix Books.
*Shrewſbury,*Mr. *DanielWillard,* ſeven Books.
Hartford, Mr. *Edward Cadwell,* Jun.
                                   ſix Books.
Brimfield, Mr. *Daniel Burt,*   ſix Books.
Sturbridge, Capt. *Moſes Marſey,* ſix Books.
Norton,   Capt. *Jonathan Lawrence,*
                                   ſeven Books.
Sudbury,   Mr. *Iſaac Baldwin,* ſix Books.
             Mr. *David How,*   ſix Books.
             Mr. *Ezekiel How,*   ſix Books.
Brookfield, *Oliver Hayward,* Eſq; ſix Books.
             Mr. *Ebenezer How,*   ſix Books.
             Mr. *Abner Brown,*   ſix Books.
Uxbridge, *John Harwood,* Eſq; ſix Books.
Upton,   Mr. *Jonathan Wood,* ſix Books.
Woodſtock, Mr. *Joſeph Chaffe,* Jun.
                                   ſix Books.

Mendon,   Mr. *William Rawſon,* Jun.
                                   ſix Books.
Townſhend, Mr. *Timothy Heald,* ſix Books.
Leiceſter,   Mr. *Oliver Witt,*   five Books.
Marlboro', Mr. *Ephraim Bridgham,*
                                   ſix Books.
Springfield, Mr. *Luke Stebbins,*   ſix Books.
           Mr. *Nathaniel Ely,*   ſix Books.

INDEX

ABENAKIS of St. Francis, capture Nehemiah How on Great Meadow, 10.
Adams, Robert, brought to prison at Quebec, 50, 50 *note*.
Adams, Berkshire County, Mass., site of Fort Massachusetts, 15; captives from, brought to prison at Quebec, 47, 49, 49 *note*; depredation at Fort Massachusetts, 48, 48 *note*.
Aikings, William. See Akins.
Akins, William, brought to prison at Quebec, 44-45.
Albany, N. Y., 43, 45, 49, 49 *note*, 51, 54.
Aldrich, John, brought to prison at Quebec, 49.
Alexander, Ebenezer, captain, marches with company to protect frontiers near Great Meadow, 9.
Almsbury, perhaps an error for Newbury, Mass., 51.
Amrusus, Indian, husband of Eunice Williams, visits How at Crown Point, 32, 32 *note*.
Anderson, Sr., James, father of James and Samuel, killed, 50.
Anderson, Jr., James, brought to prison at Quebec, 44; his father killed, 50; Capt. John McNear his uncle, 50, 51, 51 *note*.
Anderson, Samuel, brought to prison at Quebec, 44.
Andrews, Francis, dies in prison at Quebec, 52, 52 *note*.
Andrews, Phineas. See Andrews, Francis.

Annapolis Basin, Nova Scotia, vessels captured in, 40 *note*.
Antonio, a Portuguese, dies in prison at Quebec, 53, 53 *note*.
BAGLEY, Jacob, dies in prison at Quebec, 52, 52 *note*.
Bagley, William, captain, dies in prison at Quebec, 51, 51 *note*; his brother dies at Quebec, 52.
Bailey, Jacob. See Bagley.
Bailey, William, captain. See Bagley.
Baker, Robert, settles at Great Meadow, 8; narrowly escapes death by Indians, 12, 28.
Baldwin, Isaac, original subscriber for How's tract, 58.
Ball, Eleazer, original subscriber for How's tract, 58.
Ballock, Lieut. See Beaulac, Sieur de.
Batherick, Jonathan. See Donham.
Bay of Arb, army of French and Indians at, 47.
Beaman, John. See Bement.
Beaulac, Sieur de, French lieutenant at Fort Chambly, a prisoner at Boston, 33; at Crown Point, 33; subdues boisterousness of drunken Indians, 34.
Beaumont, John. See Bement.
Beman, John. See Bement.
Bement, John, brought to prison at Quebec, 46; account of, 46 *note*.
Bennet, Richard, dies in prison at Quebec, 53.

Bent, Martha. See How, Martha (Bent).
Black River, Vermont, 12; located, 29 note.
Boon, John, apprentice to Capt. David Roberts, dies in prison at Quebec, 50, 51 note.
Boscawen, N. H., formerly Contoocook, soldier from, brought to prison at Quebec, 44.
Boston, Mass., 57; How's tract printed originally at, 17, 25; Rev. John Williams returns from captivity to, 32; Sieur de Beaulac, French lieutenant, prisoner at, 33; How interviewed concerning news from, 37.
Braban, Giat. See Braband, Guy.
Braband, Guy, dies in prison at Quebec, 52, 52 note.
Brabbon, Guyart. See Braband, Guy.
Bradshaw, John, dies in prison at Quebec, 51.
Brattle, William, original subscriber for How's tract, 58.
Briant, Sarah. See Lydle, Sarah.
Bridgman, Ephraim, original subscriber for How's tract, 59.
Bridgman, Jonathan, brought to prison at Quebec, 48.
Bridgman's Fort. See Vernon, Vt.
Brimfield, Mass., 58.
Brinley, George, his copy of How's tract in New York Public Library, 16.
Brookfield, Mass., 47, 58.
Brown, Abner, original subscriber for How's tract, 58.
Brown, Timothy, letters from, delivered to How, 45; brought to prison at Quebec, 45, 46 note.
Bryant, Sarah. See Lydle, Sarah.
Bryant, William, killed at Gorhamtown, 44, 44 note; his widow married to Leonard Lydle in prison, 50.

Bryant family, 44, 44 note.
Burbank, Samuel, brought to prison at Quebec, 44; two sons of, captured, 44; wife and children of, 46; dies in prison, 55.
Burbeen, John, original subscriber for How's tract, 57.
Burt, Daniel, original subscriber for How's tract, 58.

CADWELL (Caldwell?), Jr., Edward, original subscriber for How's tract, 58.
Calwell (Caldwell?), James, original subscriber for How's tract, 57.
Cambridge, Mass., 58.
Canada, 11, 17, 20, 25, 32 note, 47, 50, 54, 56; governor of, receives letter from Mass., for exchange of prisoners, 45; proposed expedition against, 46.
Cape Ann, prisoners from, die at Quebec, 52, 54 note.
Cape Breton, 47.
Cape Cod, Mass., 40.
Casco Bay, Maine, 40, 44.
Chaffe, Jr., Joseph, original subscriber for How's tract, 58.
Chalet, M. de (written Shearly by How), interpreter of the King, visits prisoners at Quebec, 42, 42 note, 45, 46.
Chambly, fort, 12, 38, 41; Sieur de Beaulac commands at, 33 note; How and his captors arrive at, 35; number of French and Indians there in October, 1745, 35-37; origin of name, 35 note; description of, 37.
Chambly River. See Sorel River.
Chandler, John, original subscriber for How's tract, 57.
Chapman, William, captain, in prison at Quebec, 40; account of, 40 note; his carpenter dies at Quebec, 52.

INDEX

Charlestown, N. H., formerly called "No. 4," Indians at, 12, 29; Col. Josiah Willard with scouting party at, 13; captives from, brought to prison at Quebec, 43; three attacks on, 46.
Christmas, celebrated in prison at Quebec, 42, 42 *note*.
Clapp, Sarah (Leavitt). See How, Sarah (Leavitt) (Clapp).
Cloutman, Jr., Edward, brought to prison at Quebec, 44; escapes from prison, 50.
Concord, Mass., 57.
Connecticut, 54.
Connecticut River, 7, 11, 28, 29 *note*; land-grants in valley of, 8; Indian incursions along valley of, 8, 9, 10, 11, 12, 46.
Contoocook. See Boscawen, N. H.
Cook, Elisha, killed at Contoocook, now Boscawen, N. H., 44.
Corby, M., he and his wife are kind to How in prison, 41.
Crisson, Thomas, settles at "No. 2," 8.
Crown Point, fort, 12, 31; description of, 32; Indians supplied with bread at, 35.
Cummings, Timothy, brought to prison at Quebec, 45; dies in prison, 53.
Curtiss, John, original subscriber for How's tract, 57.

DAILY, William, dies in prison at Quebec, 52, 52 *note*.
Daly, William. See Daily.
Davis, Daniel, original subscriber for How's tract, 58.
Davis, John, dies at Quebec, 50.
Dayly, William. See Daily.
De Chalet. See Chalet.
De Rogers. See Amrusus.
Deerfield, Mass., 13; Indian incursion at, in 1704, 32 *note*; Rev. John Williams first minister of, 32 *note*.

Denen, Joseph, dies in prison at Quebec, 54.
Denning, Joseph. See Denen.
Denox, Joseph. See Denen.
Devonshire, England, 51 *note*.
Dewen, Robert. See Downing.
Dill, John, dies in prison at Quebec, 53.
Dogan, Michael. See Dugan.
Donham, Jonathan, brought to prison at Quebec, 49, 49 *note*; dies at Quebec, 51.
Downing, Robert, also called Dewen, brought to prison at Quebec, 47, 48.
Drake, Samuel Gardiner, estimate of his editorial work, 15, 16.
Dugan, Michael, dies in prison at Quebec, 53.
Dunbar, Robert, escapes from prison at Quebec, 50.
Dunham, Jonathan. See Donham.

EAMES, Nathan, brought to prison at Quebec, 48, 48 *note*; dies at Quebec, 50.
Ely, Nathaniel, original subscriber for How's tract, 59.
Emes, Nathan. See Eames.
Evans, Samuel, dies in prison at Quebec, 54.

FARNSWORTH, Stephen, brought to prison at Quebec, 43.
Felton, Skelten, original subscriber for How's tract, 58.
Fether, Christian. See Vedder.
Five Years' French and Indian War, 8; narratives of Indian Captivities during, 15-17, 40 *note*.
Flint, Henry, original subscriber for How's tract, 57.
Flint, Thomas, original subscriber for How's tract, 57.
Forbush, Phinehas, brought to prison at Quebec, 48, 48 *note*.

Fort, Abraham, dies in prison at Quebec, 55.
Fort, John, captain, dies in prison at Quebec, 53; his brother dies in prison, 55, 55 note.
Fort Chambly. See Chambly.
Fort Crown Point. See Crown Point.
Fort Dummer, 13, 17, 25, 27.
Fort Edward, also called Fort Lydius, French and Indians who attacked, at Fort Chambly, 35, 36; its names, 36 note; depredation at, 42.
Fort Hill, built in the Great Meadow, at Putney, Vt., 8, 41; Indians attack, 10, 11, 27; burned by Indians, 14.
Fort Hinsdale. See Hinsdale's Fort.
Fort Lydius. See Fort Edward.
Fort Massachusetts. See Adams, Berkshire County, Mass.
Fort Shattuck. See Shattuck's Fort.
Fort Ticonderoga, 12, 31 note.
Furbush, Phineas. See Forbush, Phinehas.

GALBOATH, William, dies in prison at Quebec, 52, 52 note.
Garwafs, William. See Galboath.
George II, Frenchmen swear allegiance to, 47.
George's Fort, Maine, 45; captive from, brought to prison at Quebec, 45; depredation at, 45.
Goffe, Edmund, original subscriber for How's tract, 58.
Gooden, Pike. See Gordon.
Goodman, Samuel, brought to prison at Quebec, 48; dies in prison, 53.
Gordon, Joseph, father of Pike Gordon, 50 note.

Gordon, Pike, brought to prison at Quebec, 50; his brother killed at Saco, 50; dies at Quebec, 51.
Gorhamtown, Maine, captives from, brought to prison at Quebec, 44.
Grafton, Mass., 8, 19.
Gray, Joseph, dies in prison at Quebec, 54.
Great Meadow. See Putney, Windham County, Vermont.

HARTFORD, Conn., 58.
Harthan, Jonathan. See Hogadorn.
Harwood, John, original subscriber for How's tract, 58.
Hawks, John, sergeant, brought to prison at Quebec, 48.
Hayward, Oliver, original subscriber for How's tract, 58.
Heald, Timothy, original subscriber for How's tract, 59.
Henry, Andrew, original subscriber for How's tract, 57.
Hide, Joshua, original subscriber for How's tract, 58.
Hinsdale's Fort, 14.
Hitchcock, Nathaniel, brought to prison at Quebec, 49.
Hodinhull, Warwickshire, England, probable home of Nehemiah How's ancestors, 18.
Hogadorn, Jonathan, dies in prison at Quebec, 52, 52 note.
Holliston, Mass., captive from, brought to prison at Quebec, 44.
Hoosuck Fort, otherwise called Fort Massachusetts. See Adams, Berkshire County, Mass.
Hopkinton, N. H., captives from, brought to prison at Quebec, 44; prisoners from, die at Quebec, 51 note, 55.

INDEX

Houlton, Joseph, original subscriber for How's tract, 57.
How, Abner, son of Nehemiah How, 20.
How, Caleb, the 1st, son of Nehemiah How, 20.
How, Caleb, the 2d, son of Nehemiah How, narrowly escapes capture by Indians, 12, 29; married the widow of William Phips, 20; scalped by Indians, 20.
How, Lord Charles, Earl of Lancaster, 18.
How, Sr., Daniel, brother of Nehemiah How, 46, 49.
How, Jr., Daniel, nephew of Nehemiah How, settles at "No.2," 8; captured by Indians, 46, 49; lives with a Frenchman at Montreal, 49; brought to prison at Quebec, 53.
How, David, original subscriber for How's tract, 58.
How, Easter, daughter of Nehemiah How, 20.
How, Ebenezer, original subscriber for How's tract, 58.
How, Edward, son of Nehemiah How, 20.
How, Eliphalet, original subscriber for How's tract, 58.
How, Ezekiel, original subscriber for How's tract, 58.
How, Hannah, daughter of Nehemiah How, 20.
How, Israel, original subscriber for How's tract, 58.
How, Jemima (Phips), wife of Caleb How, 2d, captured by Indians, 20.
How, John, probably of Hodinhull, Warwickshire, England, great-grandfather of Nehemiah How, 18.
How (Howe), John, grandfather of Nehemiah How, 18, 19.
How, Joshua, son of Nehemiah How, 20.
How, Margaret (Willard), wife of Nehemiah How, 19.
How, Martha (Bent), first wife of Samuel How, father of Nehemiah How, 19.
How, Martha, daughter of Nehemiah How, 20.
How, Mary, paternal grandmother of Nehemiah How, 19.
How, Mary, daughter of Nehemiah How, 20.
How, Moses, original subscriber for How's tract, 58.
How, Nehemiah, settles at Great Meadow, 8; captured by Abenakis at Great Meadow, 10, 27; his deposition to governor at Quebec, 11, 38; led to Canada, 11-13; maltreated by Iroquois at Chambly, 12; bibliography of his "Narrative," 15-17; genealogy of, 18-21; death of, 20-21, 56; writes his name on bark for Indians, 29; at Crown Point, 32; dances for Indians at Crown Point, 33; Indians quarrel about, 34; arrives at Fort Chambly, 35-37; Indians pelt him with snowballs, 36; dances for Indians at Chambly, 36; beaten by two Indians and rescued by Frenchmen, 36; arrives at Quebec, 38; sent to guard house at Quebec, 38; sent to prison-keeper's quarters at Quebec, 39, 41; sent to regular prison at Quebec, 40, 40 *note*; leads the prisoners in morning and evening devotion, 40-41; ill in prison, 41, 56; several friends of, brought to prison, 43; letters of Deacon Timothy Brown brought to, 45; receives letter from his father-in-law, 55; obituary of, 56.

66 INDEX

How, Samuel, lieutenant, father of Nehemiah How, 19.
How, Samuel, son of Nehemiah How, 20.
How, Sarah (Leavitt) (Clapp), second wife of Samuel How, and mother of Nehemiah How, 19.
How, Sarah, daughter of Nehemiah How, 20.
How, Submit, child of Nehemiah How, 20.
How family, genealogy of, 18-21.
Howard, Daniel, major, original subscriber for How's tract, 57.
Hubbard, John, captain, original subscriber for How's tract, 57.
Hull, Mass., 53.
Huntington, Sr., Hezekiah, his son dies in prison at Quebec, 54, 54 *note.*
Huntington, Jr., Hezekiah, dies in prison at Quebec, 54.
Hyde. See Hide.

INDIANS, 7; depredations by, on or near Great Meadow, 8, 9, 10, 11, 27-29; kill David Rugg, 11-12; attempt to burn Shattuck's Fort; 14; burn fort at Great Meadow, 14; method of indicating their tracks, 28; paint and erect on pole the scalp of David Rugg, 31; sing and dance around How, 31; require How to dance, 33, 36; intoxicated, 34, 35; quarrel about How, 34; subdued by Sieur de Beaulac, 34; dance around scalp of David Rugg, 35; number at Fort Chambly when How arrived there, 35; throw snowballs at How, 36; two of them beat How, 36; threaten to go against the Great Meadow settlement, 36-37; depredations by, 42, 44, 45, 46, 47, 48, 49, 50.
See also under family and tribal names for other references.
Iroquois, maltreat Nehemiah How, 12.

JONES, John, brought to prison at Quebec, 46-47.
Jones, Thomas, brought to prison at Quebec, 44; dies at Quebec, 47.
Jordan, James, captain, dies in prison at Quebec, 53; one of his men dies in prison, 53.

KEENE, N. H., 13; captive from, brought to prison at Quebec, 46.
Kincaid, origin of family name of, 39 *note.*
Kincaid, James, imprisoned at Quebec, 39, 40; account of, 39 *note.*
Kinkead, Kinkhead. See Kincaid.
Kinlade, James. See Kincaid.
Knowles, Sir Charles, 29 *note.*
Knowlton, Thomas, killed at Fort Massachusetts, 48, 48 *note.*

LAKE CHAMPLAIN, 12, 31, 34, 38.
Lancaster, Mass., 8, 58.
Lancaster, Earl of. See How, Lord Charles.
Larrabee's Point, Vermont, 12, 31 *note.*
L'Aurore, French ship, persons captured by, brought to prison at Quebec, 49, 50, 50 *note,* 51 *note.*
Lawrence, Jonathan, captain, original subscriber for How's tract, 58.
Leavitt, Sarah. See How, Sarah (Leavitt) (Clapp).

INDEX

Le Castor, French ship, persons captured by, brought to prison at Quebec, 49, 50, 50 *note*, 51 *note*.
Leicester, Mass., 59.
Leonard, Jonas, original subscriber for How's tract, 57.
Leonard, Moses, original subscriber for How's tract, 57.
London, England, 37, 40 *note*.
Lovet, Major, of Mendon, Mass., his son dies in prison at Quebec, 52.
Lovet, Samuel, brought to prison at Quebec, 48; dies at Quebec, 52.
Lower Ashuelot. See Swanzey, N. H.
Lydius, John Henry, governor of Fort Edward, also called Fort Lydius, 36 *note*, 42.
Lydius's Fort. See Fort Edward.
Lydle, Leonard, prisoner at Quebec, marries the widow of William Bryant, 50; his wife dies in prison, 54.
Lydle, Sarah, widow of William Bryant, married in prison to Leonard Lydle, 50; dies in prison at Quebec, 54.
Lynde, Judge, of New England, 39.

McGraw. See Megraw.
McNear, John, captain, uncle of James Anderson, Jr., captured, 50; brought to prison at Quebec, 51, 51 *note*.
Magra, Thomas. See Megraw, James.
Marblehead, Mass., 40.
Margra, James. See Megraw.
Marin, M., lieutenant, depredation by, at Saratoga, 43 *note*.
Marlborough, Mass., 18, 19, 50, 59.
Marsey, Moses, captain, original subscriber for How's tract, 58.
Maryland, 40 *note*.
Massachusetts, land-grants in valley of the Connecticut granted by, 7-8; schooner "Montague," commanded by Capt. William Pote, Jr., in service of, 15; genealogical data on How family in, 18-21; sends letter for exchange of prisoners at Quebec, 45; John Perry petitions government of, concerning losses, 52 *note*.
Megraw, James, dies in prison at Quebec, 53.
Melvin, Eleazer, captain, pursues Indians trying to burn Shattuck's Fort, 14.
Mendon, Mass., 52, 59.
Minot, James, original subscriber for How's tract, 57.
Moffat, Robert, brought to prison at Quebec, 46.
Montague, schooner, Capt. William Pote, Jr., master, 15.
Montreal, prisoners brought to, 42, 49, 50; prisoners from, brought to Quebec, 43, 53; scalps brought to, 50.
Morris, Charles, his map published with Pote's "Journal," 40 *note*.
Morse, Robert. See Moffat.
Munrow, Thomas, original subscriber for How's tract, 57.

Nalton, Thomas. See Knowlton.
Nantasket, Mass., 53 *note*.
New Casco, incursion at, 49, 49 *note*.
New England, 36-37, 39, 47, 50, 52, 53, 54.
New Hampshire, grants town charter to Great Meadow settlers, 14.
New Hopkinton. See Hopkinton, N. H.

68 INDEX

New York, grants town charter to settlers at Great Meadow, 14; prisoner from, dies at Quebec, 52.
New York Public Library (Lenox Library Building), depository of the copy of How's tract used for this reprint, 16, 23.
Newfoundland, 47.
Norman, Mr., captive, 50.
Northfield, Mass., 13, 14, 46.
Northampton, Mass., 33.
Norton, Mass., 58.
Norton, Rev. John, 49; account of his "Redeemed Captive," 15-16, 48 note; brought to prison at Quebec, 48; marries Leonard Lydle and Sarah Bryant in prison, 50; recovers from illness and preaches in prison at Quebec, 52.
Norwich, Conn., 54 note.
Nova Scotia, 40 note.
Number Four (No. 4). See Charlestown, N. H.
Number Two (No. 2). See Westmoreland, N. H.
Nutting, Samuel, narrowly escapes capture by Indians, 12, 29.

OWEN, James, of Brookfield, Mass., killed on St. John's Island, 47.

PARKER, Isaac, brought to prison at Quebec, 43.
Pealtomy, Indian, visits How at Crown Point, 32, 33; converses with How, 34.
Perry, John, he and wife brought to prison at Quebec, 48; his wife dies at Quebec, 52, 52 note; petitions government of Massachusetts concerning his losses, 52 note.
Perry, Rebecah, wife of John Perry, dies in prison at Quebec, 52, 52 note.
Phips, Jemima. See How, Jemima (Phips).
Phips, Spencer, lieutenant-governor of Mass., sends letter to Canada for exchange of prisoners, 45.
Phips, William, settles at Great Meadow, 8, 34 note; killed by Indians on Great Meadow, 9, 34; his widow, Jemima, married to Caleb How, 2d, son of Nehemiah How, 20; account of, 34 note.
Plaffer, Lawrence. See Platter.
Platter, Lawrence, captured at Saratoga, dies at Quebec, 43, 43 note.
Pleasant Point, near George's Fort, Maine, captive from, brought to prison at Quebec, 44-45.
Plymouth, Mass., 54.
Pote, Jr., William, captain, master of the schooner Montague, account of his "Journal," 15, 40 note; his opinion of Nehemiah How, 21; in prison at Quebec, 40; gap in his "Journal," supplied by How, 41 note; fellow captive of, arrives at Quebec prison, 49, 49 note.
Pratt, Amos, brought to prison at Quebec, 48; dies in prison, 53.
Prince Edward Island, formerly St. John's, depredation on, 47; captives from, brought to prison at Quebec, 47, 48.
Prisoners, at Montreal, 42, 49, 50, 53; at Quebec, 39, 40, 42, 43, 44, 45, 46, 47, 48, 49, 50, 51, 53, 54, 55; letter from Mass., proposing exchange of, 45; petition

INDEX 69

governor of Canada to be exchanged, 46; illness and mortality of, at Quebec, 51; isolation of the sick, at Quebec, 52.
Putney, Windham County, Vermont, description of, 7; history of, 7-14; Indian incursions at, 8, 9, 10, 11, 14, 27-28, 34 *note*; Col. Josiah Willard reconnoiters the region, in pursuit of Indians, 13-14; fort at, burned by Indians, 14; deserted region resettled, 14; new fort built, 14; town charter granted by New Hampshire, 14; town charter granted by New York, 14; organized as town, 14; Nehemiah How original settler on Great Meadow at, 19; How's capture by Indians at, 27; Indians at Fort Chambly threaten to attack again, 36-37.

QUACKINBUSH, Martha, dies in prison at Quebec, 51, 51 *note*.

Quebec, 8, 11, 12, 15, 20, 32 *note*; How arrives at, 38; prison-keeper's quarters at, 39; description of regular prison at, 40; rations to prisoners at, 40; illness of prisoners at, 41; governor at, sends money to prisoners, 42; royal intendant at, sends money to prisoners, 42; prisoners from Montreal brought to, 43; captives imprisoned at, 39, 40, 42, 43, 44, 45, 46, 47, 48, 49, 50, 51, 53, 54; deaths of prisoners at, 43, 47, 49, 50, 51, 52, 53, 54, 55, 56; snow in August at, 47; two captives married in prison at, 50; illness and mortality of prisoners at, 51; sick prisoners isolated at, 52; prison at, burned, 54, 54 *note*.

Quebec River. See St. Lawrence River.

RAWSON, Jr., William, original subscriber for How's tract, 59.
Read, Jacob, brought to prison at Quebec, 44; dies at Quebec, 50.
Read, John, dies at Quebec, 50.
Read, Josiah. See Reed.
Reed, Josiah, of Fort Massachusetts, dies, 48, 48 *note*.
Rice, Edward, captain, original subscriber for How's tract, 57.
Richards, John, brought to prison at Quebec, 47.
Richelieu River. See Sorel River.
Roberson. See Roberts, David, captain.
Roberts, David, captain, his apprentice dies in prison at Quebec, 50, 51 *note*.
Rochester, N. H., captives from, brought to prison at Quebec, 47; depredation at, 47, 47 *note*.
Ross, Aaron, original subscriber for How's tract, 57.
Rugg, David, settles at Great Meadow, 8; killed and scalped by Indians, 11-12, 28; his scalp painted and stuck on a pole, 31; Indians dance around scalp of, 35.
Rumford, N. H., 44.
Rutland, Mass., 8, 57.
Saco, Maine, depredation at, 50, 50 *note*.
St. Francis. See Abenakis.
St. John's Island. See Prince Edward Island.
St. Lawrence River, 12, 37 *note*, 38.
Saneld, John. See Smeed, Jr., John.
Saratoga, N. Y., attack on, attributed by How to Albany, 41 *note*, 43 *note*; letters to

prisoners from, brought to prison at Quebec, 45.
Savage, Edward, original subscriber for How's tract, 58.
Scaffield, Philip, brought to prison at Quebec, 53; dies in prison, 53.
Schuyler, Nicholas, captain, 42 *note*.
Schuylerville, N. Y. See Saratoga.
Scoffil, Philip. See Scaffield.
Scot. See Scott.
Scotland, 39 *note*.
Scott, Joseph, brought to prison at Quebec, 48.
Scott, Miriam, wife of Moses Scott, dies in prison at Quebec, 51, 51 *note*.
Scott, Sr., Moses, he and family brought to prison at Quebec, 48; his wife dies at Quebec, 51; his son dies at Quebec, 52, 52 *note*.
Scott, Jr., Moses, youngest child of Moses Scott, dies in prison at Quebec, 52, 52 *note*.
Scott, Stephen, brought to prison at Quebec, 49.
Scott (Scot), William, brought to prison at Quebec, 53.
Seaflower, schooner, Capt. James Sutherland, commander, 40 *note*.
Shamballe, Shamballee. See Chambly.
Shattuck's Fort, Indians attempt to burn, 14.
Shearly. See Chalet.
Sheepscott, Maine, captives from, brought to prison at Quebec, 39, 44, 50, 54.
Sheepscott river, 54.
Shepard, John, original subscriber for How's tract, 58.
Shepherd, Jacob, brought to prison at Quebec, 49, 49 *note*.

Sherborn, Mass., 47.
Shrewsbury, Mass, 53, 58.
Sinconds, Benjamin, brought to prison at Quebec, 48.
Smeed, Captivity, dies at Quebec, 55, 55 *note*.
Smeed, Daniel, dies in prison at Quebec, 54.
Smeed, Sr., John, he and family brought to prison at Quebec, 48; his wife dies in prison, 53; his son John dies in prison, 53, 53 *note*; his son Daniel dies in prison, 54; his youngest child, Captivity, dies at Quebec, 55, 55 *note*.
Smeed, Jr., John, dies in prison at Quebec, 53, 53 *note*.
Smeed, Mary, wife of John Smeed, dies in prison at Quebec, 53.
Smith, John, brought to prison at Quebec, 53.
Smith, Richard, brought to prison at Quebec, 53.
Sorel River, 12, 37; its names, 37 *note*.
South Carolina, 39.
Spafford, John, captain, brought to prison at Quebec, 43.
Springfield, Mass., 59.
Stebbins, Luke, original subscriber for How's tract, 59.
Stevens, Joseph, captain, original subscriber for How's tract, 57.
Stone, Jonas, original subscriber for How's tract, 58.
Stone, Nathan, original subscriber for How's tract, 57.
Stoughton, Mass., 58.
Stratton, Ensign, takes part in pursuit of Indians near Great Meadow, 13.
Stroud, William, from South Carolina, imprisoned at Quebec, 39.

INDEX

Stubs, Richard, brought to prison at Quebec, 49.
Sturbridge, Mass., 58.
Subes, Richard. See Stubs.
Sudbury, Mass., 18, 19, 58.
Sunderland, John, brought to prison at Quebec, 53.
Sutherland, James, captain, commander of schooner Seaflower, in prison at Quebec, 40; account of, 40 *note*.
Swanzey, N. H., captive from, brought to prison at Quebec, 45.

TAINTER, Benjamin, brought to prison at Quebec, 53.
Tainter, Simon, lieutenant, his son in prison at Quebec, 53.
Taylor's Island in Connecticut river, 11.
Tedder, Christian. Se Vedder.
Thayer, Jonathan, narrowly escapes capture by Indians, 12, 28, 29.
Townsend (Townshend), Mass., 59.
Trent, Capt., killed, 54.

UPPER ASHUELOT. See Keene, N. H.
Upton, Mass., 58.
Uxbridge, Mass., 58.

VADER, Christian. See Vedder.
Vanderverick, Geret, dies in prison at Quebec, 51, 51 *note*.
Vaughan, Samuel, dies in prison at Quebec, 54.
Vedder, Christian, dies in prison at Quebec, 54, 54 *note*.
Venhon, Samuel. See Vaughan.
Vermont, 12.
Vernon, Vt., depredation at, 46 *note*.

WARREN, David, brought to prison at Quebec, 48.
Warwickshire, England, 18.
Watertown, Mass., 18.
Westborough, Mass., 49, 53.
Westmoreland, N. H., formerly called "No. 2" settlement of, 8.
Wheeler, Thomas, original subscriber for How's tract, 57.
Wigglesworth, Rev. Dr. Edward, his autograph on copy of How's tract used for this reprint, 16.
Willard, Benjamin, captain, father-in-law of Nehemiah How, 19; sends letter to How, 55.
Willard, Benjamin, original subscriber for How's tract, 58.
Willard, Daniel, original subscriber for How's tract, 58.
Willard, Josiah, colonel, commands scouting party near Great Meadow, 13-14.
Willard, Margaret. See How, Margaret (Willard).
Willard, Samuel, original subscriber for How's tract, 58.
Williams, Rev. Eleazer, great-grandson of Eunice Williams, 32 *note*.
Williams, Eunice, daughter of Rev. John Williams, married to Amrusus (otherwise called De Rogers), an Indian, 32, 32 *note*.
Williams, Rev. John, captured by Indians in 1704 at Deerfield, 32, 32 *note*; returns to Boston and publishes account of captivity, 32 *note*.
Williamson, Jonathan, captain, brought to prison at Quebec, 54.
Windham County, Vermont, 7, 27 *note*.
Witt, Oliver, original subscriber for How's tract, 59.
Wood, Jonathan, original subscriber for How's tract, 58.
Woodstock, 58.

INDEX

Woodwell, Daniel. See Woodwell, David.

Woodwell, David, brought to prison at Quebec, 44; two sons, daughter and wife of, captured, 44, 46; his wife dies at Quebec, 51, 51 *note*.

Woodwell, Mary, wife of David Woodwell, dies in prison at Quebec, 51, 51 *note*.

Worcester, Mass., 57.

Wright, Noah, his account of attack on Great Meadow, 10 *note*, 11.

www.ingramcontent.com/pod-product-compliance
Lightning Source LLC
Chambersburg PA
CBHW051706090426
42736CB00013B/2567